LIFE IN

A BOX

IS A

PRETTY

LIFE

LIFE IN
A BOX
IS A
PRETTY
LIFE

DAWN LUNDY MARTIN

NIGHTBOAT BOOKS
New York

ISBN: 978-1-937658-28-1

Designed by Mary Austin Speaker

Cataloging-in-publication data is available
from the Library of Congress

Distributed by the University Press of New England
One Court Street
Lebanon, NH 03766
www.upne.com

Nightboat Books
New York
www.nightboat.org

What strikes me is how easy it is to commit atrocities.

–KARA WALKER

MO[DERN] [FRAME] OR A PHILOSOPHICAL TREATISE ON WHAT REMAINS BETWEEN HISTORY AND THE LIVING BREATHING BLACK HUMAN FEMALE

After Carrie Mae Weems's Framed by Modernism (1996)

To feel a presence, they say, can be like a haunting. You are yourself and no other physical being is there, yet a feeling or sensation emerges as if from nowhere. Like The Negress. The black female body not in repose, instead walking or clickity clack. It knocks at the door, which is the surface of existence. Or, in life, it walks down the street and is asked to assume a position of slackness in response to the perception of being in perpetual heat. What would we do without her? How would we know our selves? Indeed, we need something against which the pristine can manifest itself, can create its artifice of pristineness.

To be unadorned

    or unclothed—light bursts—

Glare from fluorescent mouths breathe their profit into me. [No one hears the glass sound of breath, just me.] Was "low," they say, "fastened in place by violence." Was "ritualized" was "debased" was "grotesque" was "black flesh" or "swathed" in "blackness," and "finality" and "nature," was "sensualized."

          In standing repose, the object lures us into a belief that she is indeed human. We know this from her sun-draped eyes, her capacity for deceit. We see no absolute proof, however, against the artist's outstretched offering—the mammy trophy and "the fantastic Al Jolson performing his signature tune!"

Enter machines and abstractions [zip!], automations to lengthen legs, round edges, plump buttocks. Relational fish, irrational fissure. All this shimmery ache in one place, suddenly against your back. My body aflame with it, can't you see? Make an outline around my form. Use your chisel. I will indulge your every little fit, I, your perfect muse, your ██ ██, your everything, also your nothing.

Insofar as the phrase "black woman," re-place outside of domestic "power." I lie down in the ditch myself, stretch my body alongside the dead myself. Outside the frame, oblique lover (de Kooning, maybe, as a young beauty), his hand reaches in to retrieve me, and pets me, my nakedness, a fine scratch. Filament traces in the historical body.

Representation falls away. Chokehold "blackness." Swallowed "brown." Your "black" father whose "blackness" precedes him. Stumble in laborious "black" gait toward "absence." Cross your "black" hands, empty your "black" pockets, hold your "poor" "black" baby against "brick" "wall" as instructed. And the "niggers" get "sold" up the "river" against a "lithe" "white" "fluff." You wail a mimic-mouth into beaded rhythms of us-ness, fragrance of a cosmos where roads are not partitioned. No roads. No marks to mark up the whole big wide world, the holes of universes untethered from time. In absence of wholeness catch glimpses of the sides of selves.

If we could be without him we would. Is there any country without him? We are told of the reservoirs, that they are without sea or wind, that we attach, laconic swerve, and hold what has happened there. Trauma sack. "What strikes me," she says, "is how easy it is to commit atrocities." Remove from experience, rain, un-nurture the physical form, a girl is just a girl, one ass cheek on a full chair, balancing, remove skin, water, sunlight, love, position the neck so that landscape dissolves into black wall, excise language puffs from pharynx, unfurl the scroll, hear ye hear ye.

WE ARE _____ WITH GLEE

When dissonance occurs go to the back of the line. When it ratchets itself up, jump into the river. Mammoth voice is our voice, the other side of illness. And we are always here, the mother with a jar of hair grease, her provocations to keep you well. In the woods you'll hear a fire, but there is no fire. Hold onto the photo of the girl in a pale green dress. Require less sustenance. Crush your strings into a single acre.

OH, SUSANNA, HOW THE SUN SETS ON THIS LOVELY LAND

Da-dee da-dee tee dee—place where cavernous—ta da ta dee dee dee. In the square, we drink iced coffees, bam bam, pow pow. One more cervesa. Otro everything. Ship workers in from wherever. Let them maintain our harmony, our fortitude. Fold happy hands in grace. It feels so good to be here.

A thriving sea even though it's sick, and everyone's kind of sick too, huffing landscapes of junked cars and computer keyboards. I'm wary. My mother is not the person I used to know and one night I cry into stitched silence, and again later when it's hot under blankets, turn to face water, or I am in water, dream of drowning returned. Irina says poems always have birds in them. Or dreams always have drowns in them. The dog is so strong in this one, I cannot protect him. Say again we could not know the limp of decades, and the body waves, a giant flag in wind, your face becoming my face. Goodbye again. It's colonial logic, really. There are things here we desire. Resources. Drip into lapis and full like light is full, all my media meaningless in this light, a strange farce, the weapons you know, unexpected. Seer says, *of* but not *from*—

In here, it always smells of burning wood and rain.

My status is ruptured. Sensation of a black boy walking.

[   ] [   ] [   ] [   ]

When you wake your ass is bare. [Your door is open.]

When you shit yourself. [Parades!]

How to register the junket in the current condition. Think of the tiny placid form. *Hey, girl, hey hey, come to me wholeness and fresh.* A narrow vile of wilderness. Then, factor of dissembling. What it does in split. I speak to you from a crack in the surface, from the elongated scar, a silver cylinder.

Fortress upon me [the I in dramatic gesticulation, its façade trembling]. When the soldiers come, and they will come, it will be important to note know objects of particular use:

"fatback" "your lard loins" "rivers"
"my father's black uniform"

When, later, the fold is undone, no memory—

Form arrives at the end of language.

[The body in the basement is bobbled with welts. It cries and cries in a wet corner. We must leave this in the well.]

"Representation just fell away."
"To liberate the past from the past."

Whispers, "my father's cold lantern," "brown and grey dickeys."

Memory, the absence of thought.

Pull all hair from comb.

Fold into square of white paper.

Set fire over toilet.

When we were kids every day.

Nothing.

Knees tugged together, when no light, pale purple dress pulled down to hem knees to cover, someone distance mouth pinch hum, silent hum, not a song but a series of sounds or grunts, black flies in the backs of throats. In this photo, the yard is safe. The other one is demonstrative in its affections. You inhale wet air, feel lonely as blue shoes are lonely, grime there, to reach into the open mouth and pull out a foreign substance, a bone or a lock. I know nothing about the yard, I say when questioned, bare souls undoing themselves.

Some try to tell us that reading is the same as living, but we know this is not the case. The letter is not a breath. Even the body's cells are contrivance. Or accidents. Floating screens: black bodies, unfathomable, violent acts. Only Will Smith has been spared. There is writing and then there is this cut, this whelm.

When I, a lad, swelling and succumbed, no one spoke to me—dripping. They tell me, I should lurk, shoulders cast forward, bullish. Shudders pelt into braced maw. She sent me a mauve dream, and I thought the words "cracked open." All the wolves—what we might produce in shadows for fawns.

HELLO, FREE HOUSE, HELLO.
NO, GOODBYE. SO LONG, BUZ
ZARDS   WHITE EYE
D
GHOSTS.

Critical assessment, relative closeness—unfortunate box—rigid, no pliable formula in the divide. To avoid catatonic state, glaze in hole of what's not left over. They say there are traces, that there will always be traces. It's a fiction anyway, a construction of the mind's needs—that they hold onto filament gestures as material. In the hole, we'll find a digging, fingernails deep in refuse. Here is the trash heap, nothing there except a muted wailing. The orator is on the horn. The orator is telling his life story. We walk the long hot sidewalk toward water. Touch, here, is imperative. To hold up contact, contact of suspense and wanting, to prop up or sustain, to call into being from elsewhere or a reminder of access.

Lake, interminable. I do not know where my house is. Where is my house? Summer steams by. Every border is cocked and ready. Flatten body against cool earth. Lie without sound. Be a cool corpse under wire teeth. The police are so young. They do not hear the wailing. Wailing, I'm told, is a figment of your imagination. What to know of the body's refusal to open, of its hidden cave? Put the cave inside another cave so no one can reach it. Perspiration aches. Strain against dirt walls. I have come to you from a metal house. We had steel barriers to protect us from the sun. The lake drifts into forever. Windows here are small and I cannot see myself in them. What it is to be captured without spoons.

We never took the train to Sayville and then the ferry to Cherry Grove. We will never go to Cuba. Instead, entered a state of impermanence. Hard to wear down hard corners into curved juice. You say, I totally don't care, which I take to mean the night sky is beautiful but I'm cold. Contortion fits. Wants air, wants treetops. Wants to touch, cannot touch. Never took a night train, bed into small bed, hovering up above many rivers. (Seek elevation.) I am driftwood. Now, the crux: I opens promise heaps. (Impossible opening.) A wrangling of desire into a paper hole. Wacky constriction. The I stuffs hands in pockets and walks a small circle. What else to do? Can't afford any new clothes to get fabulous. When the seer said, you might be a completely new person in a year—

Life inside grid object, replace faces with armored ducks, drive off fucking cliff, get all damaged after raging. What holds the structure: giant ministries, giant everything! They don't want you to hang yourself. Instead you survive. Spring is here! Let's poison the grass to make it shine. We are shiny people. If you were to hang yourself, you wouldn't die, you don't know how to die. Hurt calm at edge of bay. Today, calm not choppy. Who's digging inside the earth for wooden faces? Super structures of defense lined up outside your window. *I'm happy!,* you sing. Register at the desk, indicate whether you understand sentences.

The American middle class is screwed again but they don't know it. Politics is a gleaming nowhere. Žižek fantasizes about Capitalism's inevitable end. Reviewers want these poems to be more hopeful. Love is obvious. She's a tutu shelter leaning out! Love is miraculous. She's twirling quite naturally! We dangle our feet in a July swimming pool. Shoots sparkles from eyes—to quiet to quiet all our little monsters. Street habits rear up. Any fire. Any quell. Who's made it to well being? The television projects hysterical grief. Brown women wailing fall to knees draped over. We are only who we are supposed to be. No moon tonight, dear one.

Dear one, the sea smells of nostalgia. We're beached and bloated, lie on shell sand, oil rigs nowhere seen. It's Long Island and the weather is fine. What to disturb in the heart of a man?

A boy is not a body. A boy is a walk.

Shed the machine.
Must be entirely flesh to fight.
Must be strategy instead of filling.

What to disrobe—centrifugal logic, as in here is a slice of my finger. Tell me the circumstance of your dick extension. When we slip into imprecision, we lose control, windowless walls close in. Awareness of being in a female body is a tinge of regret. "The human frame to adapt itself to convention though she herself was a woman." To receive, to be entered, to fret around upon entry. It's grand. I'm a system. Plants tall as wheat to hide in.

When blanched in suspension.

When turned white from irons.

When hung by one ankle.

Hails knocks down midday. It's beige.

A black arm extending out.

Without fodder. A voice plays
background, saying:

A body is a piecemeal accumulation. It's already fraught. We attempt
to construct wholeness. No debris. No breaking off eastward.

To button up in a tight gray sweater what has been released.

Want to be in your limelight. Want your limelight to coo. Birds coo. Or coo coo. Want your clock to be rocked. Press gentle against opening. Resist entering. Hold cake inside mouth. There's standing to be done, cage ripening to tend.

Order, we know, is love. Without clothes the body feels its own flesh suddenly. To imagine fear when it's not present is to evoke the erotic, is to prepare a cool wet cloth on the body's surface, a cleansing, a room is tied down, a single chair as anchor. Feet flat against tile, tied ankles to chair, legs open and relaxed. Notice a faded spot in the wallpaper, a distant sound outside the window. *We are challenge. We are devout in action.* Here's the thing about being a prisoner, it's transformative. Daytime brings a fat robin, merciless in its presence. Everyone is dreaming again.

Life in a box is a pretty life, arrangements and things. We all have the same type of feeling. There's some drifting. *Breathe into my bag.* Flowers. To fight is to lie down among the dead. [Unstable space.] [Claims historical.] History is littered with severed cocks. A want to be buried there—those ruins. *Things seen from the corner of the eye occasionally indicates a wider haunting.* Gapes to fall into. Almost everything we've ever desired is diminished when enclosed. Attempts timelessness. Attempts prayer. Can find no god, no oracle, no air. This is concavity. Feel cut of skin darkened in such emergencies. Who wants a strobe light ring? Who wants a pickle? Small comforts. Hapless encounter on the subway or after a show, and we squat down inside ourselves.

When the head is shoved it naturally resists. Covers her dark face in a black cloth (could be a hood).

WHEN WE ARE INSIDE THE PRISON
WE CAN ONLY THINK OF BEAUTY

We are infinitely disgraced. Wishes, well-wishes, eel. I am eleven and am and let into a dim room where my brother and his friends are watching a 32 mm film in which a woman is gangbanged. Upon entering the I distends. To claim is to maneuver. Punishment referent: belt, whip, glory. *We speak to each other through mountains. You excrete god likeness. Whose presence entered my world? Who decided upon and then let go? I present you with a phantasmagoric me. I wear a sheath and jewels. My tits hang out. I'm unworthy. Mouth unfastened, draw in. I fast. I work. I design. I craft. I lend. I pour out. I stiffen upon command.*

Power is exercised where it can be exercised. Exacting precision. Spectacular momentum. Ninety-nine percent of the time, the ones in power will act like victims, will say, *We're not in power, we're trying to save all of us, it is for the sake of order. The current conditions are unforeseen.* They will say, *It's not our fault*, or *We didn't notice. How can we notice when the buildings are burning? We're doing everything we can,* they'll say, and, *Our hands are tied.* Bayonets already positioned. Figures in white, shadowy, through smoke. They appear to dance in half time. Jangle-mo. Distracted by concretions.

Squeezes legs rhythmically, hopes no one notices. This is better than love because it is not unlike pleasure. No way to fill, no persuasion in the effort of filling. Relentless hours. The Global Economy is killing me. My mother tells me the story of Sodom and Gomorrah over again on the telephone. Has she imagined sodomy? Has she imagined flesh filled and flesh ripping? The state of things in the state? It's a broad sphere of unsanctioned doings. When I'm at my lowest I feel just fine. No money in my pocket, crouching behind the abandoned broke down carousel. Head-severed horse whinnying for me. *Where are you? he calls. I dreamed I'd forgotten your name.*

Historically, we extend. We drift into. We are back straight. We bind. We draw. We categorize. We are punitive with regard to fairness only. We are method. We are order. What would you do without us? Oh, we are so very smitten.

This morning I had a dream and remembered it. In the dream, you are ill and in the hospital. Maybe you're dying, I don't know. I think you are pocked and leper-like. It doesn't matter. I was so worried about you. I answer my phone. It is not you but a friend who rattles on, who cares about what. The inevitable box makes an appearance. Tonight he's shiny—fetching, one might say. *I was inside of the reverberation, beyond exhilaration.* How to learn consensual violation? Feels in the mouth like—cannot explain—has an image of—you are probably thinking of some kind of particularly dinosaur-like bird that dives into the ocean and is relentless in its pursuit, opens beak, throat for fish.

The body an upright suit, designed as intent. Smooth over belly filled with unsafe duck meat. Leniencies follow. Enter the building with your special pass. Checkpoint around skin. The black apostle comes to me in a cowboy hat. *Dear angel,* I say, *I cannot fuck you tonight, my father is dead.* Button shirt up to collar. [Being in love with the pitch of experience means one must wear a common cloak.] [Violence stuns the body into submission.] How to know what violence is? Always inches from disappearance. From swelling into unrecognition.

If we could come to you we would. Assistance is in our nature. We are without motive. But we must operate within constraints. Fresh as new leaves. This is our approach. The wall is not a blockage or a guardian but an alignment. An alignment is an affection. An affection is a twist in the loins. Which we, in all our wisdom, know is the right thing.

HOW IS A MOUTH
SUPPOSE
D TO OPEN WILLIN
G   LY?

Which demands from the incident? All reservations on hold so that the skin might ache properly. Integument listener. Volumes and ink and inquiry and yet, no face against the written. We have learned that progressing is a quiet thing.

A desire to rip the bottom out of experience—these bodies, they say, are ungovernable.

IT WILL HEREBY BE OBSERVED THAT NIGGAS
GET SHOT IN THE FACE FOR THAT MENACING,
THREATENING LOOK!

I, now, a dead woman. Hunt leaves as might a child. Swing up through my own lack, my own chaos. Hurt staged in the lung. They ask me of the paralytic, of the collapsed upper aperture.

But what of this human need, mouths my mute.

The I radiant in heat, polish. *I am closing my legs now.*

Subsiding against graffitied wall, pinched to
hold up—

This negro type
is ancient. The
Egyptian monuments
demonstrate its
existence four
thousand years
ago. Unless the
physiography
of the
landscape changes
profoundly, the
negro type will
probably exist
here four
thousand years
hence.

Land divides despite the shine of skin, opens itself infinite, or a howl.
[Too many bodies to count.]

Or how wonder works. When I am squatting to retrieve a cup of
vaginal blood, and bearing down, as the instructions say, as in
defecation, I am wondering.

Industrial children held—

Territory forgotten—

Territory bludgeoned—

—*Why are all the children bound?*

—They are all musicians.

                                    Continual
                                    mouth
                                    breathing can
                                    affect the inner
                                    ear.
                                    Without good
                                    hearing the
                                    controlling
                                    factor of
                                    correct attack
                                    and good
                                    pronunciation
                                    is lost.

Their pleasant asylum—

And which contains?   Entertainments—

Shaken mumbled something   was—

supposed to be names—   Translated—

In whose service the pet—

—A kind white woman—in whose service—rescue—

It is wonderful the volume of sound that seemed to be hidden away in
those small dusky bodies.

In the dream, the black dog sobs and cries Mommy, his hurt so profound he cannot stand. His legs splay out across the linoleum floor. My brother has all of his teeth removed after significant rotting. We fist pump at the game and hoot. The sobbing becomes the air. We close storefronts, drop down to ground, pull our knees up to face. Agitate, the microphones say, but no one moves.

To padlock circumference of the neck.

When they said they'd split me in two, I was overjoyed, wanting to get at the rip of things.

How to inhabit the sensation of living.

We are without allegiance. We are royal in our independence.

When the I speaks, it speaks into an other's speech. This is a labor. Next to her, a learned man is gray and wearing comfortable shoes. He does not think about the shoes, he simply wears them. He seeps. It's impossible to determine the monument of his instructional value.

They can't figure out why the rapes keep happening.

Blood point of needle. Carnal hovering. It is we who say, "they were protected" and at the same time "fetish."

Yet,
fecund
plump]
pink-like
or
heavy
omission—
dare
to
god-dread
[body-panoramas]
blurred
constitution
[an avenue]

I, between teleological mishaps, evident national orders. Another thing, entirely, to be a mother. Open gull mouth. Stuff in charcuterie. Forlorn is the limp of neck gazing up.

Am border state body marked. Body as scene.

O, happening happening, refuse melody, I open my unfit beak, its perfect script, the wide nostrils agape for proper channel of admission.

You enter the space, your body is approximation form, its sensibilities /

There are supplies
of all sorts on hand—
quinine, calomel,
hypophosphites, and
even cod liver oil are
some of the remedies
that keep the little
colored orphans and
half orphans and
destitute children in
proper physical
condition.

Red surface bumps. Speed up wind property.

Am before marked. We, the only evidence.

To be a nice whi— whu— is, perhaps, to be the nicest thing on earth.

To be in memory, destructive impulses,

a worship in the side room of the mind.

--

Survival skills liturgy:

Except, who was taken? We want to imagine our connections like sweet water.

Except, the possibility of complete missingness of the person.

All the time now, on the streets, beings suddenly laughter, bursts of grief roll, indiscriminately limp fits.

Sometimes in spite of myself, the word, God.

A book is nothing, they say.

A want to theorize this phrase but then flesh just gone.

Tisa tells me about the coming dirt shortage.

When the I speaks accosted—

Excerpt from temperament (one is not allowed temperament). Especially for a body that is already gesture, an antagonism, a wig. The most threatening physique is wiry. Something felt in the reaction to it, a feeling as in an imagination, or a creation, or a repetition. Feeling is lodging. A human living form that is a bark. My wood barks into the night, strains, holding in consumption. Your pink bubbly babies are safe. Everyone is safe. Which is an offering and which is a laceration?

THE MAIN CAUSES OF THE EXODUS WOULD SEEM TO
HAVE BEEN POLITICIANS, RAILWAYS, AND LAND AGENTS

It doesn't matter. You just present yourself or happen in the room and perspectives all around you. A glassy eyed woman tells you to hush. A tall man takes your cocktail from your hand and tosses it into the trash. Excerpt the noun and place it next to a vowel. Wreck your immediate world and watch the aftermath. The walls of the room are white and short. In it, you claw because there is nothing else to do. Who's listening? The portrait of the man framed in gold leaf?

It's not the word "body" that's the problem. It's the physical thingness of it, the hump.

For thousands of
years there lies
behind the race one
dreary, unrelieved,
monotonous chapter
of ignorance, nakedness,
superstition, savagery.

When we encounter the savage, we are in reverie. This is precision joy, concomitant stroking. Are you me? Is this our jackal face? O, I love it, I love us. Let me make a comparison. The jackal face akin to my father beating me with a soup spoon, I'm so unruly.

Without invitation, the I is left to encounter an aged woman, all her useless parts hang from the falcon's mouth. Chasm of impertinence to exist so lackluster, draining out.

> After a vaginal
> examination they
> determined that her
> uterus was enlarged,
> her vagina over-
> abundantly moist, but
> her long and "tumid"
> clitoris was the tell tale
> sign of nymphomania.

I look up into your void and experience crisis. Rapid formulations on the screen and in it some other kind of genius you don't understand the medical therapy or the ways the East Village has more rats than other places in the city.

Bleeding and caustics   understand
          bloodletting

          Cooling baths   strong emetics or bleeding as tangible
demonstration

Resolutely   genitals   that women's   overworked
          undernourished

hearth crucial.   Wombs. My mother's womb!   *All your
diseases come from*

your pussy. This is logical. When my mother braids my hair she
stuffs my head down into her netherworlds. Capacity dominated
their entire
being. Shaped

          citizens determined men's lives.

Lie down. *It's illegal to lie down under duress.*

Stiffen. *It's against the law to stiffen when being attacked.*

Instead, to be quartered and—

Rip off—and trying so hard not to remember—

Locality—rendition of hardness—

From before, they say, "my father" and "had no vocation"—

and—"labored"—"work horse"—

Because the black—which race is God, no one asks—we are very
hearty—in the space of irreconciliation—you know, my father,
worked 16 hours every day, never complained, never got sick, went to
work with a dearth arm—*What if they posture sadness?*

I was illustrative, an example angled toward proof. I was biologically female but that was of no use. Whose holes are these, begs one. Another dives into the being and refuses to come out. This is the invalid position. A wakening in the spirit of another.

The Irish, the
Iberian, and the
Negro are of
low
prognathous
type. Less
petting and
more
disciplining is
needed; fewer
academies and
more work
benches.

What is the sound of sounds

sounding indefinite fist in face again and

sound of the surprise of it coming

from nowhere, of breaking the arm

on a small fall in your own house,

a respiratory failure, wound opening like a little mouth.

We inhabit the brutal. We are shattered every day.

We look askew. Head broken floor array, light

array, great distances, life goals.

Staked upon every border,

guardians. Protections have many faces.

Misuse of the face as a streaming

desire. Solution posted: "Get rid of all the niggers."

The state exacts its controls.

That the pepper spray happens against kneeling children—

That the search for the secret leaker is unyielding—

If you want, you can make a myopic focus, concentrate

on a shone shadow or drift off into space.

This tendency,
if persisted in
will probably
in the end prove
disastrous
to the advancement
of the colored race,
since there is
but the slightest
prospect that the race
will be lifted to a
higher plane of
civilization.

Girl, tell me, how did you come here? You are supposed to create a situation in which belonging seems imperative. Better, perhaps, the hovering between borders until the hole opens and you see a tiny crystal inside your gut. For days I feel a small knot in my bladder as if carrying something. They say it's nothing. Girl, you are not beautiful like the others, your hair, everything—it's that magnetism I seek. To secure us, we hear of foiled terror plots, other threats to the nation.

The length of a body suffering, the length of my vacation swimming pool. Crisp wake, pop pop, tatters fall from sky. This is a phenomenon worldwide. The sad psychic sends you non-urgent notes as if to say do you mind me telling you things. How the blood holds or does not hold—

Apollo Belvedere
Negro
Young Chimpanzee

I insertion into vagina. When the rains come, we hear unmemory cloaking its needs. Wants to burst accordingly akin to wire tugging at gum-teeth. Keep the lips shut, the wicked say.

To treat the nation as threat is to lose one's head. Recent studies show thousands of nation people dying of loneliness. These trajectories account for several difficulties in repairing out-of-control germs. The primary attempt is exhaustive fucking using as many household objects as possible—a retreat into some measure of innocence. To close the distance between the abject and bliss.

Which of our distinctions bears unreasonable resemblance to other noticeable features? Alternatively, phenotypes. Body draped as marquee. Despite the fact that they want us to desire "a regular mode of living," we satiate the silver cylinder and tighten.

We labor in our attempts at rebirth. Remain inside enclosure, wood box.

Felt mostly in legs becoming sausage pipes.

We stand, again, with our heads hanging outside apartment windows, hope to catch breath, to redo trained breath, heavy quick work.

We expect the baby deer to die before a certain age.   Who—

Willing force. Food security.

On corners, the despised Jehovah's Witnesses in bad suits and conviction. A window, they say, and draw the shades.

I will not sing to you. I refuse to sing to you.

WITHOUT KNOWING THE SLIGHTEST THING ABOUT WAR, I FIND MYSELF AN INSTRUMENT OF LABOR, INVESTIGATION, AND EXPERIMENT

What are the dimensions of the field? They've put me here in the tallest grasses and strangest fruit and have demanded at gunpoint that I bend into it over and over, but I'm so tired, and my limbs are sore, and I feel disconnected, or I disintegrate, a shadow figure towers over me as I exhaust, body buckle, ballast removed.

When the dirt is black enough, when my hand is strong enough, I dig into it, open space, and fall through other side, to a black sound, a black stone, familiar thieves, Urdu or the last language we spoke before mother's milk. They circle around me, clasping wrists, and I yell into a hole in the earth in earth, my palm proffers Oromo, undoing silt—break away.

This is the body bending over my body. They have encircled me with their manacle tongues, but I do not understand them. My form is small and lean but they think I am large and bull-eyed. What is yielded here is nothing. No sign of blood, no sign of dripping, no ache, only my small form without space around it. What is the body but a leaking form? No room for leaking. A form so tight around my form it cannot seep or gesture. Complete enclosure.

To hold a drop of water is extreme labor, tongue against ground, the difference between experience and dreams falls away. There are locks in every corner like little eyes. Even time no longer passes, each fractured second redundant, artifice of time, of location. My father's red eyes—

If there is a wandering I do not know it, the eye-lock has its determinant grip. When I open my mouth someone else speaks words that happen in my dreams as islands.

Jaw agape, a work of wheezing. Each day to the river, but dry. Weight of crackling. In the hand, a mass of grandfather's thin hair, wind mass: a voice speaks soft into ear, says *irretrievable*, says, the dog too cries *Ma-ma*. Hair, a spare mass of grief. How to make the self distinct amongst white whales.

A dead fawn under machinery. I am the machinery. Am also the end of the sentence. In heat, they want me, also to lap at their crotches saying thank you because their syntax wants definition of this body. All the colors. It is you who are they. From inner valve, an Orphic effort, a monument force against your greed feast, your half-lidded gulps. You ruminate, you vomit into the mouths of fawns. You say, I love you, I love you.

Wound resurfaced, unlocks, a face in my hand, white sinews visible. It startles—this flesh against skin, a reminder but for tree depths, I can see them, my reflection, stone black as ice, bulging body, a root to depth. Obscured by hammer of whiteness. Organs collapse in bright fortress.

My form removed from its home, its warmth and sustenance. They tell me I have enough, that I am not dying, but I see my own gray legs ashen. To witness the floor, and then it's me on the floor. Carry the draped body feet-first, already a hole forked, my spirit confused from return. The slaves blink their slow eyes. They pull their tie-knots close to collars—dead wings, faces bald—and speak with ease. Boom, the voices go—my head, an empty vase.

They will tell you that I was sick, that I was a drug addict.

They will tell you I died a natural death. Sometimes young people just die, they will say, we don't know why. They will say I was lazy, that I could not work because of disease and just general feebleness. When a crime is committed by a white man, they will show you a photo of me instead and call me a trickster. In the photo, my jaw is slack, my hair wild. They will say that I am unkillable, that my body resists battery by tree trunks, bullets, and years in small cells. When I enter a store to buy something I will be immediately arrested and then they will apologize. I am just a child I will say. Impossible to be so greasy and a child they will say there are no children anymore. Why are you so sad, they will ask me, why is your heart so weak? We've given you everything, they say, why won't you flourish?

The slaves are dressed as men. They go to work in gray suits. Their bodies are grammar incarnate so they bracket force when inside gated halls. They contain themselves in bright photographs that refuse speech. They partition the doors to prevent interlopers. Sometimes they use the word *savage* when the containers leak.

Repository.   Chemical doorways.   Many Armies.
Fragrance glut. Plume.   Vine-torn.

Where are my hands and feet?

Where are the lights?

In here! In here! I'm right before your eyes!

Fuh fu—

        f-f faw   blue   red   twinkle

CODA

25 TINY ESSAYS ON THE VALUE OF FORGETFULNESS AND SLEEPINESS

Proust proposes, using a Celtic belief, that souls of the dead are "held captive in some inferior being, in an animal, in a plant, in some inanimate object, and so effectively lost to us until the day (which to many never comes) when we happen to pass by the tree or to obtain possession of the object which forms their prison. Then they start and tremble, they call us by our name, and as soon as we have recognised their voice the spell is broken. . . .And, it is so," he continues, "with our own past. It is a labour in vain to attempt to recapture it: all the efforts of our intellect must prove futile. The past is hidden somewhere outside the realm, beyond the reach of intellect."

*　　*　　*　　*

1.
We are told about excavation as ideal, about release and demons. The fragrance of knowing.

2.
I mean to write the phrase "the body in trauma" but first I write the phrase "the boy" to refer to me, and then I write "the body is trauma," never achieving my original intention.

3.
The I is collecting documents in her body. *Why are you writing me?!*, it bellows.

4.

Is always *after*—production from things that linger or lean back into. What is the nature of before as in the sentence has not yet begun?

5.

Not just cellular matter or excretion. The phrase in my ear, "I've always wanted to fuck a black woman." Silver platter donkey.

6.

Push her backskin against tree bark. Don't care. Feeling feels good at any rate.

7.

Body as concavity. As excitement. As instigator.

8.

I is the stabbing wound intellect. Wound as in puncture, not wound as in spindle.

9.

There are incidents the I cannot remember or does not want to remember. Eleni and HR indicate that the body is an archive. I think I believe this. But where does it go, memory? Memory as adumbration. Is this fear?

10.

A garage in the middle of nowhere filled with beer cans ordered high in stacks, labels facing out, long as laces.

Slipping now.

11.

If absent from happening, if unbound by discovery. Have coveted dissociation. The body as a construction of miniature vaults. I imagine them to be perfect cubes of thick shiny steel. If the work is an investigation it is an investigation into the horrific, the terrifying, the unknown.

12.

A body like this one but much smaller than this one. Somewhere.

She. She wake she. Black. Is all.

13.

Sometimes you find little handwritten notes in your own handwriting and you do not remember writing them. They say things like, "None of the structures are helping." And then the phrase "HAUNT BUBBLE" in all caps like that, which you like.

14.

What has been born into?

15.

"Death space," I want to say when Frankie asks where in my body does writing begin its habitation. "I do not know," I say instead. And then I see a figure standing in the middle of the stage: a reflection of my own form. My head is severed from the rest of my physical form and floating there, and my eyes hover outside their sockets.

16.

It is you who shudders to be opened.

17.

To be awake, alert, on guard, might be to miss the very thing that shimmers just beyond what's visible to the attentive eye.

18.

The limping subject wanting so badly to know itself. Exalted space, now, clamoring.

19.

The idea that the physical form is just one part of the body and that we might instead imagine the body's imagining of itself.

20.

Splitting occurs in aphasic scribbles and destroys the world of the self. To recover is to bring forth betweenness. What's left over?

21.

In the female form the writing comes from what femaleness? These are saturated geographies that have been over-tended to. Here is the white female body carved from white stone, unreachable. Here is the black female body with a mammy hat. These geographies want for a certain neglect.

22.

To be liberated from the wakefulness state itself.

23.

Unwritings as unravelings or unwindings as in to become undone, to reach the edge of sleep, and balance there, not noticing but loosening.

24.

I want to happen past a tree. Happen past to find the souls of the dead there, trembling, the obliterated selves I once thought were locked inside the imagined body's miniature vaults.

25.

Storehouse bombed. Vaults empty, just vaults.

NOTE

This work incorporates some borrowed and/or manipulated and/or erased language from late 19th-century ideologies and texts including Frederick Starr's "The Degeneracy of the American Negro"; J.L.M. Curry's "The Negro Question"; and, Frederick L. Hoffman's *Race Traits and Tendencies of the American Negro.*

ACKNOWLEDGEMENTS

Many grateful thanks to the Montclair Art Museum for the opportunity to spend time alone with the collection in residency, which brought my meditation on Carrie Mae Weems's work into being. Thank you to O'Clock Press for publishing *The Main Cause of the Exodus*, the chapbook in which several of the poems in this collection were first included and to Wintered Press for the first publishing the chaplet titled, *Order.* Versions of poems were also first published in *Mandorla*, on *The Volta*, and in the groundbreaking anthology *Troubling the Line: Trans and Gender Queer Poetry and Poetics.*

I am deeply indebted to the HOWDOYOUSAYYAMINAFRICAN? global artists collective, particularly Sienna Shields, for inviting me to become a member and write the libretto for the opera, *Good Stock on the Dimension Floor*; poems from this collection were initially put to music and performed by the gorgeous multitudes of the YAM Collective.

I am so very lucky to be surrounded by so many brilliantly creative people, not limited to, but especially, the Black Took Collective (Ronaldo V. Wilson and Duriel E. Harris) the East Hampton Writers Project (Stephanie K. Hopkins, Kristin Dombek, Nicole Callihan, and Marion Wrenn); and Liz Latty, my first and closest reader.

Deep gratitude also for the institutional support from the University of Pittsburgh and the Can Serrat Artists Residency.

And, to my loves—I'm forever not just grateful, but awe inspired by your generosity, your openness, your willingness to, with me, alter the material world and make new shapes. Nothing would be possible without you.

photo by Thomas Sayers Ellis

DAWN LUNDY MARTIN is the author of several collections of poetry including *A Matter of Gathering / A Gathering of Matter* (2007) and DISCIPLINE (selected by Fanny Howe for the 2011 Nightboat Books Poetry Prize). She is a member of the Black Took Collective, an experimental performance art/poetry group of three, and HOWDOYOUSAYYAMINAFRICAN?, a global artists collective. An Associate Professor of English at the University of Pittsburgh, Martin is currently at work on a memoir.

NIGHTBOAT BOOKS

Nightboat Books, a nonprofit organization, seeks to develop audiences for writers whose work resists convention and transcends boundaries. We publish books rich with poignancy, intelligence, and risk. Please visit nightboat.org to learn more about us and how you can support our future publications.

The following individuals have supported the publication of this book. We thank them for their generosity and commitment to the mission of Nightboat Books:

Elizabeth Motika
Benjamin Taylor

In addition, this book has been made possible, in part, by grants from the National Endowment for the Arts and the New York State Council on the Arts Literature Program.

ART WORKS.
arts.gov

State of the Arts
NYSCA